The Not-So-Fun Ride to School

Łukasz Marek Sielski

DEDICATION

To all small and big commuters

ACKNOLEDGEMENT

This book is crafted with a primary aim to engage and educate parents rather than children. Through the lens of a child's perspective, the story unfolds, offering insights into the longing for meaningful connections amidst the challenges of daily life.

Designed as a catalyst for discussions, the narrative touches upon themes such as spending quality time together, effective time management, awareness of risks and dangers, and the shared responsibility within a family. It serves as a gentle and calming tool to initiate dialogues on these important aspects of family life, fostering a reflective and constructive exchange between parents and caregivers.

As you journey through the pages, take a moment to reflect on your own experiences and consider the behaviors observed on the road, both yours and those of others. Use this story as a starting point for brainstorming how to make your family's travel experiences more enjoyable and safer.

Encourage self-reflection, as personal insights can pave the way for positive changes. Spend some quiet moments contemplating the narrative on your own, and ponder how it resonates with your family dynamics.

For additional guidance and information, please refer to the end of the book

Not-So-Fun Ride to School

Okay, so like, every morning, my mom and dad take me to school in our big, cozy car. It's super warm inside, and I like it 'cause it's not all wet like outside. But, you know, I get kinda bored in the car.

I wanna talk to them and tell them about my awesome dreams or my new drawing, but they're like, "Shh, sit quietly." And that's no fun!

Sometimes, they drive really fast on this super twisty road, and it makes me feel like we're on a roller coaster. But I get scared, especially when they start yelling at other drivers. I'm like, "Are they mad at me too?"

And guess what? They're always looking at their phones. At home, in the car, everywhere! It's like, "Hey, look at me, I'm here!" But they're too busy with their phones. And then, they're like, "Why are we late? Stupid traffic!" But they never ask me how my day was.

One time, I saw some kids trying to cross the road in front of our car, and my mom didn't see them 'cause she was too busy looking at her phone. That really scared me! I was like, "Mom, watch out!" But I didn't say it 'cause she always look so mad.

I see other kids walking to school with their parents. They're holding hands, talking, and smiling.

Some even have cool scooters or bikes. I really, really want to ride my bike to school with my dad, but he says it's too busy and dangerous.

But guess what? I saw a super cool bike lane near the other school!

just wish we could spend
more time together like
the happy families I see.
Maybe we could talk and
laugh instead of being in a
big, quiet car all the time.
That would be super
awesome!

.

SOME FACTS FOR THE PARENTS

Hey mom and dad,

I wanna tell you some important stuff, not just my made-up stories, okay? I love you so much, and I want you to be safe.

First, no phones in the car! Even at the red light or in a line, it's not cool. You can get in big trouble, like fines or losing your license. Even if you use the loudspeaker, it's not safe. Scientists say you lose attention, and you might not see my friends or my teacher on their bike. Don't do it, okay?

Our car air is not so good. Bad stuff stays inside, and we both breathe it. Even electric cars make yucky particles from wheels and brakes. Not good for us!

Speed signs are not targets, they're

limits. It's scary when you go too fast. Why risk it with me?

The lady on the bike is my friend's mom. She's going to work. When you pass too close, it's scary for her and us. You can get a ticket, too. Give her space, and if we can't pass, we can wait. No rush!

Don't complain about cyclists not paying road tax. Mr Churchill got rid of it, and now everyone pays for roads with taxes. Our car messes up the road more than their bike, same as an elephant would more than an ant.

Thanks for listening, love you!

Your kiddo

Printed by Amazon Italia Logistica S.r.l.
Torrazza Piemonte (TO), Italy